no one leaves the world unhurt

no one
leaves
the
world
unhurt

JOHN FOY

AUTUMN
HOUSE PRESS
pittsburgh

"Autumn House Press" and "Autumn House" are registered trademarks owned by Autumn House Press, a nonprofit corporation whose mission is the publication and promotion of poetry and other fine literature.

 Autumn House Press receives state arts funding support through a grant from the Pennsylvania Council on the Arts, a state agency funded by the Commonwealth of Pennsylvania, and the National Endowment for the Arts, a federal agency.

Text and cover design: Chiquita Babb

ISBN: 978-1-938769-75-7
Library of Congress Control Number: 2020947432

For Majô, Catherine, and Chris

Contents

one

two

three

four

five

one

the payment plan

You, too, will be officially enrolled
in what we've come to call the Payment Plan,
     and while it's true this isn't optional,
our policyholders will, we think, attest

          that parity is what we're aiming for.
The plan is quite unique in that you pay
     in the universal currency of pain.
Our actuaries first consult the charts

          and calculate, for someone of your age,
the ratio of grief to be applied
     based on tribulation indices,
and then a consultation is arranged.

          One of us will come and sit with you
to individualize a strategy
     that fits what we believe you can endure.
We have a range of policies we think

          are competitive in the marketplace of woe.
Despite our best advice, some people ask
     about the Harvard Plan. This plan ensures
that all affliction comes immediately

          and overwhelmingly to guarantee
that you'll go into shock and soon forget
     your password and your mother's maiden name.
A DNR is included in the plan,

and you can choose ahead who pulls the plug.
But this is probably not the one for you.
   We understand you have a narrative
that helps impart some meaning to your life.

      Well, who would ever think it otherwise?
We're open to most every point of view
   and can contextualize, on a sliding scale,
the water board, the billhook, and the drill.

      Installments every month are preferable.
We urge you to avoid delinquency
   and hope you know that interest will accrue,
as per the plan, on unpaid balances.

alan kurdi

There is no interest at this time, no hope,
   no place that isn't far away.
Please help me, if you can, to understand.
    I don't know what to pray for now
that Alan Kurdi lies there on the sand.
    It looks as though he's had enough.
There's nothing now that I can say to him,
   a little boy upon the beach,
face-down. He lies there at the end of time.
    His days upon the earth were few,
and water was the final thing he knew.
    His shirt was red, his pants were blue.
Now let me go to him and pick him up
   and take his body in my arms.

report card

I got a B for being there
because I wasn't really there
the night my father died. I was
on business down in Baltimore
and got the message back at home.
I'd been with him that Saturday,
but I was in the hospice, then,
in spirit only when he died.
In sadness, well, I got an A.
It was a mandatory class.

I got a C for taking care
of animals—a dog I had
—but there was nothing I could do
when she was taken by disease.
She went from chasing after deer
and swimming in the Delaware
to lying crippled on the floor
and left on pentobarbital.
I took her body to the car
and got an A in bitterness.

I got a D for doing what
my mother wanted me to do
when she was in her final years.
I gave her all the time I could.
I kept the books and went each week
to see her in a nursing home
that was supposed to be the best,
though it was not a place I'd want

to have to smell for very long.
I earned an A in sorrow there.

An F is what I got for faith.
My prayers were not that regular,
and once a year I went to church,
a failing in the eyes of those
who like to monitor such things,
but if you think of pain as prayer,
why, I've been at it constantly,
and were I graded on that curve,
then I would get an A and know
that I had earned the grade I got.

gollum

You poor son of a bitch,
corroded and ruined in the dark,
down there in the deep mines.
You creep out of the caves now
to limp and lurk around the fens
and grab out fish to eat
or lay hold of a few rats.
Big-eyed and blasphemous,
closer now to the amphibian,
you make a mockery of those
who pity you, and letting go
was not a choice you ever had.
Your sad story was only about
the earth and what was in the earth.
It wasn't peace of mind you sought
or any equilibrium.
What did comfort mean to you,
who spent five hundred years or more
ruminating underground
on what you did and didn't have?
Who else but you could know so much
about deformity and pain
and what it means to be alone?

making war

The shelling, never final,
blew out his mind, and we had to go
and light up that bleeding fighter in the ditch
and bring him down closer
to his pool of blood. We'd fire
and forget that this was being.

What was it like, being
shot to pieces? It was not final
right away, raked by fire
in the rain, but no one could go
and drag his entrails closer
to the safety of a deeper ditch.

We spent time in drainage ditches
or whatever holes we could dig, being
dogged and shot at, always closer
to the dirt geysers and the final
gate through which we knew we'd go
into the bone-ends and rain and fire.

The stinking heat from gasoline fires
kept us warm in the ditch,
and no one thought he'd die and go
to heaven, those thoughts being
held at bay, even amid the final
things, the blue brainpans, always closer.

The enemy was always closer
than we'd thought, pouring down fire
on our flanking team, and then a final

blast and bewilderment in the ditch,
the last they knew of being,
and then, all undone, it was time to go.

There was nothing to do but go
and try to get in closer
to the berms, a rush being
the only way, then, to mount fire
and shred them in the ditch,
where the degradation was final.

We all had to go into the fire
and come in closer, up against the ditch,
being ready for what was final.

into the mountains

What's to be done, and who really cares?
We are far from what we know, and the nights
out here are cold, the stars beyond anything
we'd ever seen back home. Killing time
is not the wasting of what time we have
but the wasting of whatever sets
its will against us.
                    It is them we waste
when we find them, when we go
to get them in the night, when we hit them
in caves with thermobaric bombs.
We get them time and time again, but again
they come back, and again, and what's
to be done, really, with those who dwell
deep in the mountains of Afghanistan?

under fire

Rounds are coming right at you,
right at your four-man fire team,
from a point about a hundred meters out.
Look to your front for gullies and ravines
or the hulks of burnt-out vehicles,
for you must go to them now,
running toward what only wants to kill
and dump you at oblivion's door,
neatly or blown open, it doesn't seem
to matter how. Your time has all come down
to a cooked and shot-up piece of some machine
covered with blood, O Holy Mother of God.
But what forgiveness here, for what's been done?
The gunner and the gunned-down are one.

cordite

It's not like what you hoped it would be.
You must get to know
intimately, like your daughter's voice,

the sound of different vehicles
and the shriek and crack of all the types
of rockets and rounds coming in

all around you, everywhere,
in the bowel-evacuating fear,
and you must know the common smells

of gasoline and campfires
and the smell of cordite and deodorants
and how to crawl backward with a gun.

clip

Get used to the lack of light
before going out alone
on night operations to do

the work the night is given to.
Find a place that's safe and dark,
perhaps at the far edge

of an assembly area
or an unlit rally point,
and sit there quiet and open-eyed

with a full clip clicked in
until you've grown accustomed
to the weight of the weapons.

concussion grenades

You have five of these
concussion grenades, four fastened
to your ammunition pouch

and a bastard in hand, like a baseball.
Look at the target, gauge the range,
and line your body up with what

you want to hit. Remove the clip
and pull the pin. Then throw
it, overhand, and follow through

the way a center fielder would,
like Carlos Carela did that summer
when he nailed a runner at the plate.

two

prayer

It came to us, though likely by mistake.
We'd never made a contribution
or given any sign to indicate
a commitment or position.
I read the flyer in the dirty cold,
in that corridor of yellowed walls
with a seatless throne at the end.
"No representative of ours will call,"
it said below the prayer.
"Should you so wish, we will not seek
further contact." They took such care
to prevent our feeling ashamed or weak,
the prayer mailed in a plain envelope
to hide the hopeful, compromising words.

cup

I don't believe or disbelieve but think
of how we're given to barbarities
and what it would have meant to him, a drink
of water then, a wooden cup to ease
the pain he must have felt, the agony
of holding up too long a cross that played
his flesh and marked him as a deity
along the way of grief he took that day.
The thing is, no one leaves the world unhurt.
I like to think of him, a stick in hand,
scrawling words or something in the dirt
that people might or might not understand
who come to hear what truth he has to tell
but bring no cup of water from the well.

one hundred pounds of myrrh

for Joyce Polistena

You knew her simple name and called to her,
allowing that we often make mistakes.
That night, she thought she'd seen the gardener.

You looked upon the coins of Lucifer
and took, withal, what you had come to take.
You called to him, as you would call to her.

You lay amid a hundred pounds of myrrh
where few can tell what is and isn't fake,
and there you were at night, the gardener.

But what is truth, and what were you to her?
Some nights, not even Peter stays awake.
You knew her name, and so you called to her.

You were the one who so few thought you were,
but just a word was all that it would take,
and what then does it mean to be a gardener?

Look how bad we've been and what occurs
when Peter, too, is sleeping at the gate.
The words you uttered first were just for her.
Then. Forever. Now. The gardener.

contemplative

for Chris Childers

The birch I point to, even though it's late
to practice any kind of augury,
is right in line with that old apple tree
I look upon beneath the sky and take
my bearings from. It's here I sit and wait,
though who knows why, to see what comes to me
—a crow could be a sign of penury
        or something worse to contemplate.

What happens in the temple of the trees
when wind comes through, as if at will, I'm left
to figure out, and then a flight of birds
across the blue above this property
I try to read, but tell me, who is fit
        to fix the flying into words?

coyotes

Coyotes at night,
even here, cannot forget
the ends of the earth,

coming back with news
of what it might mean to go
hysterically mad,

unless that's the sound
of what it's like to end up
never coming back.

the veery

A *million trillion billion.* That's the song.
It isn't loud and doesn't last for long.
It's only heard at twilight, in between
the night that's coming and the day that's been.
The one who sings out where the woods are wet
has kept the distillations of regret
in crystal vials and pewter pipes, a bird
that knows the first waters of the world.
It's then I go outdoors and try to sheave
my memories of you here and believe
that maybe there is no such thing as wrong
and all we have to do is sing our song.

wheelbarrow

in Brejal

This one has had its share of woe
if the chewed-up look of it
is anything to go by now.
It knows a little bit about
all the washed-out nights of rain
and summer days, just standing there,
in the sad, tropical sun.
Blue moons have come and gone,
and hell has frozen over thrice,
and work, the sweat of big hands,
has educed, somehow, a shine
from this life that's mostly given
to dirt and dust and firewood.
The barrow's been relied upon
to take on stacks of cut-up wood
for the bonfires we often light
and sit by, talking for hours
in the soft Brazilian night.
It's been relied upon to hold
itself together, wheel and pin,
and not give in to grieving much.
It's known some better days, and worse,
like us—no mystery there.
It stands behind the house,
obedient and filled again
with wood that we will use tonight
to build, again, a bonfire
here under the Southern Cross.

leaving são paulo

The wing at night, the stars,
a navigation light
blinking at the end,
and the ailerons pulled in,
at peace, whispering
that this is all we are.

out of body

My body died. I saw it from above.
I drifted out of it, and there it was,
like something used. I looked at it
on the gurney, trying to be sure.
All was bright and very beautiful,
like when you see someone you haven't seen
for a long time, you want to go to them.
My mother was there in the energy and light,
and I saw the faces of my son and daughter
not wanting me to go, but not afraid.
And that was it. It happened years ago
and doesn't matter now. I have some friends,
a few who still come by to sit with me,
but it doesn't matter anymore.

night riff

I like to sit in the dark and play guitar,
going for some of the dirty grit and chime
that steadied me for years, like medicine,
like whiskey in the woods. The dog's awake
and wondering why I'm here, but that's okay.
The sound is quiet, rich, and sure enough
to soothe the mind of any animal,
and when I play, I usually close my eyes
to better test how fast my fingers find
the notes I should have gotten long ago.
The dog, a dog I love, is back to sleep,
and I am left alone with my guitar,
as much of it as I can hope to play
without a thought for where I have to go.

three

funeral

No word really rhymes with *funeral*.
There are, though, some that almost rhyme,
like *useful, futile, irretrievable.*
And then there's *tuna casserole*, but that's a stretch,
and *urinal* is inappropriate.
I do like *brutal, crucial, cruel,* and *doable.*
And what's wrong with *denial?*
The director of a funeral home
told me I would leave this *mortal* life.
He was beyond *contemptible,*
but that was long ago, when my father died.
He sold us bogus death certificates
that were, for *legal* purposes, not *usable.*
His cufflinks were *incomparable.*

the stinker

Although it's all the rage to question now
a common human nature, let's concede
at least a brotherhood that's based on how
each one conforms—and does the daily deed.
Like everyone, the democratic man
assumes that very fundamental pose
ennobled by Rodin, whose thinking man
conflates the art of thought and the repose
of one attending nature's dividends.
Hobbled by urges rude and execrable,
the body in allegiance has to bend
but won't forsake the form of the ideal,
a posture of the highest in the base,
that man might lose his load but not his face.

it is what it is

It is what it is.
It's not what it might have been.
It's not what it had been.
It isn't what it could be.
It's not what it ought to be.
It won't be what it might have been.
It was what it ought not to have been.
It will be what it ought not to be.
It ought not to be what it is.
It's surely not what it was.
It can't ever be what it had been.
It'll never be what it could have been.
It ought never to have been what it had been.
It was what it was.
It's not what it was.
It is what it is.

the haunted mansion

for Robert Sandor

The Haunted Mansion in Long Branch, New Jersey,
employed locals with hatchets and wigs
to function as psychoneurotic lunatics.
For us, Holy Mother of Christ, it was bad

—the locals with hatchets, wearing wigs,
coming at us down the dark hallways.
O Sweet Jesus, it was bad,
and it didn't help that we were tripping on acid

as they came at us down the dark hallways.
How bad could it really get?
It didn't help that we were tripping on acid,
and down you went to the floor, in shock.

That was how good the bad could get.
To think that we had paid for this,
and there you were, on the floor, in shock.
That was certainly real enough,

but this was what we liked. We paid for it.
You'd said, back then, "I wish that I were me."
Now *that* was real, or it was real enough.
Our Haunted Mansion burned down years ago,

and I, too, wish that I were me
and with you again on that pier tonight,
but it burned down long ago,
the Haunted Mansion in Long Branch, New Jersey.

the partridge family

I hate the fact that every Friday night
I watched *The Partridge Family* on TV.
I fell for it. They travelled in a bus,
that family band, and did "performances"
in Caesars Palace or back in the garage.
It was a family show, a lot of cheese,
and so the single mother, Shirley Jones,
would smile and sing but never did get laid.
It would have been that fellow named Kincaid.
He was the iffy dude, their manager,
played by David Madden, who was not
averse to making guest appearances
on *Love Boat*—let us speak no more of that.
My problem was I actually believed
the Partridge Family played their instruments.
Do you remember David Cassidy?
He looked like he had eaten vaseline,
but Danny Bonaduce was the worst,
and Danny Partridge, the character he played,
was a little douche bag with a bass guitar,
as charming as a lump of soda bread.
He shuffled around in a psychedelic shirt.
In later life, the actor got involved
with drugs and lived inside a car behind
Grauman's Chinese Theatre for a time.
He was arrested once, in Phoenix, for assault,
when he punched out "a transvestite prostitute"
he'd taken for a girl. Now, that was bad.
For Danny Bonaduce, it was real.
For me, the time I wasted Friday nights
watching the Partridge Family play the songs

they couldn't really play was not ideal.
What good did it do me in the end?
I even used to know the lyrics. Now
I'd rather drink a beaker full of Fleet
and go to get my colonoscopy
than be reminded of the matching vests,
the tambourine, and Danny's red guitar,
and how, back then, I thought it fit and meet
that such as these should sing of happiness.

headless barbie commission

What a cheap, plastic piece of shit.
But it comes with a certificate

—"of authenticity," no less,
to put whatever doubts I had to rest—

printed on heavy stock to make us feel
the Barbie we just purchased is the real

deal. Our doll, the piece of paper tells,
was made by "artists at Mattel"

in Indonesia, and it's true they look the same,
but why break the mold or change the name

when product sells? Besides, it reassures
to know that what we bought is just like yours.

A more put-together girl-next-door
is sort of what she is. But *caveat emptor*!

The unblemished, budding little Venus
doesn't have a heart or anus,

and although she has a cute rear end,
her svelte little body doesn't bend.

(Who could blame her if she stiffened up when
she knew she'd have to spend her life with Ken?)

It's uncharitable, of course, to say whore.
She's supposed to be a girl, nothing more,

and there's no telling what I'll have to spend
on accessories—world without end!—

because accessories are half the fun
—*in saecula saeculorum.*

God help us. And please don't speak of love.
We're only talking dresses, hats, and gloves.

My daughter, Catherine, still a child,
is already starting to see the lie

in Barbie's upbeat, catatonic face
gazing across all time and space.

In collusion with her brother, Chris,
quick to see when something is amiss,

she has formed the Headless Barbie Commission.
(He helped to formulate the mission.)

They line up every Barbie doll she's got,
and in the name of what is real and what's not,

they set about their task, and Dad is glad.
They pull the heads off. (Ken is sad.)

boxer shorts

My boxer shorts were made in Vietnam,
and there they are, at Walmart, on the shelf,
but from what hands? A woman's or a man's?
Or was a child impelled to work? Myself
I sing. I do not have the luxury
of time to think about the ones who make
the clothes I wear. They do it overseas.
Presumably they're paid and get their take.
In Southeast Asia, labor costs are low
for Hanes, the GAP, and even L.L.Bean.
It's what we know, and all we need to know.
My shorts won't creep and have a double seam.
If I don't like what's in my Value Pack,
well, I can go and get my money back.

it's not ok

I get it, but it's not OK
bigot tike stint out
it's not, but OK, I get it
bike ousting tit tot
it's OK, but I get it not
obtuse ingot kit tit
it's not OK, but I get it
stinkbug tie tit too
I get it, but OK, it's not
bikini test tug toot
I get OK, but it's not it
tube tooting ski tit
it's not, but I get it, OK
bittiest gun kit too

going mad

I'm cleaning out the cracked house of my mind.
The first to go is "O I love my life,"
since now I only hear a bluto bag
wheezing in the infundibulum,
as though I weren't a citizen at all.
It took a little while, but now I know
it is the planet Pluto that I am,
a dwarf in orbit in the Kuiper Belt,
a coney in the deepest cold and dark.
It's not so bad, although it isn't great,
to be a ball of frozen nitrogen
—I miss my shitty, broken clarinet.
There's nothing left to say except that once
I went about with wits in Witchita.

unlocking the incredible power of small stones

The 7 Habits of Highly Effective People
The eight traits of likeable folk
How to live authentically in Cleveland
Here we go—coming to terms with self-immolation
My lifelong struggle with Sambuca
A grifter's guide to Penn Station
Come home, Pappy—the lost years in South Dakota
The book of neuroplasticity for homeless men
I'm Albanian. How 'bout you?
Grandma's cup of quarters—growing old in Vegas
How to talk to very young women in Brooklyn
Burmese meditation for alcoholics
You've got Crohn's Disease—now what?
Three hundred ways to lose your job
How not to fall in with harlots and fornicators
St. Anthony and the hermeneutics of masturbation
How old is too old?
Ringo Starr's big book of bright beads
Al Sharpton and the Kama Sutra—the end of history
Donald Trump and the Kama Sutra—the rebirth of tragedy
Digital rectal exam: techniques, insights, and epiphanies
How to manage your feelings during wartime
A young woman's guide to gels and ointments
Take it from Gumby—life without a penis
How to meet single mothers in Albuquerque
A libertine in leotards—anatomy of a midlife crisis
Mortuary science, depression, and sexuality
The 98 most dreadful ways to die
Smegma—the medical dictionary for young boys
How to stamp out your old personality

A few drinks after church—Jesus & gin
Cognitive behavioral therapy for Bolivians
Climbing Mt. Everest at 95—a short story of hope and personal tragedy
A coward's guide to intramuscular injections
Last call—becoming who you are in a hospice
Why do small Korean gymnasts have to die?
Enemas and eremites—colon-cleansing in the Early Christian Church
How to start your own funeral home
A year in Lithuania—my life as a sexual acrobat
How to get along with others in a federal penitentiary
Spanky's guide to end-of-life decisions
Unlocking the incredible power of small stones

four

the museum of sex

233 Fifth Avenue, New York, NY 10016

i

I'd like to go, but who would go with me?
Not everyone, of course, is up for this.
My wife has called it a redundancy
and said that I should go with David Katz,
my poet-friend, but David's not inclined
to visit such a place, just him and me.
Would there be dioramas like the kind
at the American Museum of Natural History?
To go alone would be unthinkable.
How sad, to wander through the galleries
inspecting things that don't seem doable.
A group is probably best—a coterie
of seven poets not so free from sin.
I wonder if they'd even let us in.

ii

Our poet-friend and sculptor, Meredith,
was happening up Fifth Avenue one day,
and there it was. She went inside forthwith
to see how certain things might be portrayed.
The gift shop—well, that's where she ended up.
She saw *The Little Book of Big Breasts*
and guides to New York City swinger clubs.
Who would buy these books? The other "guests"
were mostly in their twenties, and in groups,
and Meredith was not that comfortable.
Which ones, she thought, had shaven off their pubes?
The shop was fun but not that memorable.
The net effect was nothing but ennui
for one who truly loved anatomy.

iii

The days went by. I hadn't been there yet.
My life is tricky, maybe much like yours.
I work a job, I try to pay my debts,
and when the weekend comes, I do my chores.
What is it, anyway, about this place?
Who cares about the Museum of Sex?
It's not a space that all consider safe,
and much there is inside that intersects.
If you have eighteen dollars, though, you're in.
It isn't funded by the NEA
and doesn't need to be. It's a win-win.
The secret is that hanky-panky pays.
A business plan, you ask? You needn't fear.
The public antes up to enter here.

iv

My wife, at last, agreed to go with me,
and I was glad. She knew that I had planned
to try and conjure up some poetry
—erotic and obscene. I'd try my hand.
Much wiser now and having sown our oats,
we wouldn't feel ashamed at being there,
but then she asked if I'd be taking notes.
This gave me pause. I will admit I care
about appearances. So how could I
take notes in a museum such as this
without a fear that one might ask me why?
These things, for me, aren't easy to dismiss.
But then my wife suggested—good for her!
—that folks would likely say, "Oh look, a scholar."

v

(After having been . . .)

A major disappointment, this. I'd hoped
to see outrageous paintings on display
or installations with machines and ropes
and groups of tantric acrobats at play,
the brave transgression of performance art.
There wasn't anything about frottage,
no enemas, and nothing on the squirt.
Not even an exhibit on massage.
There *was* the "Kinesthetic Camping Ground,"
"A Thousand Years of Chinese Imagery,"
and something called a self-pleasuring tent.
But three copulating elk? That took the crown
and undermined, a bit, one's dignity,
although I guess I'm glad to say I went.

It might have fallen short in some respects,
a house of only curiosities,
but nothing there was not involved with sex,
so one was spared from true monotonies.
The John Boy doll, aghast and well prepared,
with orifices opened up like Os,
had found himself, well, closer than he dared
to something called a Pleasure Periscope.
I saw the penis gourd, so primitive
it didn't look to be much fun at all,
and then The Juicer Chair, prohibitive,
that featured on its seat a six-inch dowel.
The Virtual Girl we will not soon forget.
She wore a horse-tail butt plug and a net.

vii

Unrivaled here, my wife agrees with me,
was *The Uncensored Story of the Natural World*.
Well bless my soul! I never thought I'd see
a Spanish ibex frightfully aroused
and flexible enough—*oh dear*—to get
its member, Twizzler-like, into its mouth.
It looked so self-sufficient and content.
And what about those hedgehogs going south
—fellatio! Now *this* was news to *us*.
An Asian couple stood there pondering
the organ of the black rhinoceros,
appalling in its length and wandering.
The thing most recognizable, to me,
was two baboons in coital ecstasy.

viii

Most hard for us to understand was this,
the homosexual necrophilia
of mallard ducks, a monstrous kind of bliss
unheard of even in Slovenia.
One went on record—*please*, I kid you not
—engaging thus his dead friend on the shore
for sixty minutes till the money shot.
Abhorrent! Take me home. There can't be more . . .
but wait. The pornographic bonobos!
Next to them the Japanese macaques
are almost saints. The lively bonobos
inquire into everybody's cracks.
A caption says they often run amok
and mount whichever one is out of luck.

ix

The Tijuana Bible, that was rich
—amusing some, demeaning many more,
a book of filth, according to the Church,
with images of clerics, nuns, and whores.
What *was* that cleric doing to the nun?
The drawing wasn't altogether clear,
but we could see her habit was undone.
Was that a hand upon her naked rear?
The drawings of a wayward Donald Duck
implied he had unspeakable desires.
What villainy it took to make him quack!
Poor Donald. Even he was in the mire.
The Tijuana Bible—cheap and fun.
Back in the day, I might have gotten one.

x

What to tell the kids? That Mom and Dad
agree the "ass-lock" isn't very nice
and "monkey rockets" only make us sad,
that these are the epitome of vice?
The less that's said the better, in this case.
They would, I'm sure, be mortified to think
we paid to walk around in such a place,
and who can doubt they'd end up at a shrink.
That's probably what we'd have to pay for next.
They're still too young to realize that adults
are often keenly interested in sex
despite the fact we look like shuffling dolts.
After such knowledge, what forgiveness?
We've led our loved ones into the abyss.

xi

Majô, my wife, was underwhelmed. The place
was funny, yes; sophisticated, no.
Venetians knew about erotic grace,
like Titian, Veronese, Tintoretto
—suggestion was the beauty of their art.
But here? The animals were a surprise,
those bonobos, the rhino's private part . . .
Everything was right before our eyes.
That Asian couple showed up once again,
I don't know how, inside a room with us.
They looked our way, and we, too, looked at them,
and then we got out quick, all four of us.
Nothing there was warm or intimate.
My wife said this, and I agreed with it.

If Socrates and Phaedrus were around,
they might've had a thing or two to say,
especially Socrates. He would have frowned
upon the John Boy doll. While not dismayed,
he would have disapproved. He'd surely note
that in this place the hapless charioteer
would see his one good horse come down with bloat,
leaving the other horse—the bad—to veer
toward the copulating bonobos.
And thus the charioteer is led astray,
away from heaven down to things below,
where wisdom often hasn't much to say.
If this is where we're destined, let's at least
explore a fitting way to feed the beast.

xiii

A minute more, perhaps, with Socrates?
He'd say we feed upon the food of semblance,
the half-real *nourriture* for such as these,
the fallen ones, like you and me, entranced
among unrighteous and degraded things.
The food of which he speaks, they have it here.
The gift shop is replete with it: a string
of Dirty Fortune Cookies we can share
with friends; the Penis Pasta, that's unique,
as are the labial pods of marzipan.
Not even Zabar's matches this boutique.
Confections here will tempt the Son of Man.
Let no one tell us that we'll go to hell
for buying edible Jo Atomic gel.

xiv

Envoi

It's Christmastime, a time to purchase gifts
for those we love: my two sisters and brothers-in-law.
So back we went, my wife and I. What if
we *bought* a few of the curious things we saw?
Those Pussy Sours, they would score some points
with Paul and Angelo. The Gummy Bears
shaped like penises are not for saints,
but Jennifer and Penny wouldn't care.
And lo! My wife observed two elderlies,
older than us, at least, at the vibrator table.
A store clerk spoke to them, explaining these,
telling them as much as he was able.
The woman held a big one in her hand
and made some reference to "the promised land."

five

the television set

We hauled it out of a neighbor's garbage pile
and carried off the booty to our fort,
Johnny Bowman and I, when we were boys.
Our fort was a refrigerator box
deep inside a wooded corner lot,
and this, our treasure, was a Magnavox.
We carried out a small experiment
and bashed the screen in with a baseball bat.
The glass erupted fundamentally.
Inside were gizmos wired to their boards,
the black, cylindrical capacitors,
resistors with their little colored bands,
so many that it took the breath away,
and wires that we gingerly picked apart.
Each component was invested with
the mystery of those things we didn't know,
but each held out an incremental hope
that we might learn, one day, just what it was.
We divvied up the ripped-out circuit boards
and figured other boys would covet them.
We had an iron poker with a hook,
a diabolic thing that Johnny got,
and this we'd use upon our enemies
if they so much as came to look at us.
But the enemies that summer never came,
and so we had to make the best of it
alone in our refrigerator box,
guarding with a poker what we thought
was worth the time we spent protecting it.

long live rock

I lived for so long in that edifice,
that house of decline, where all my dreams
of rock stardom, never really mine,
existed like radioactive ghosts,
hyperexcitable and glamorous.
Electric guitars, I thought, would redeem
the dying I endured behind machines.
But that redemption never came to pass.
Instead, hysteria. The rock idols
fell foul of their dead counterparts, the ghouls
from that old film where failures walk the earth,
and there was disembowelment and betrayal
in the psychic house of the incredible.
My labor was no more than it was worth.

the bank

Before our livelihoods went down the drain,
Everyone said it's all good and that,
At the end of the day, there is no end of the day.
Risk reigned. We were good to go.
So, going forward, how appalled we were
To see things going backward, downward badly
Every day, what we worked for dumped
As damaged goods for the greater good of all.
Ruin whispered in the very word
No one cared to look too closely at:
Subprime, bad, a bad end
Just waiting to occur. And when it came,
Pulling down a venerable house of cards,
Mostly jokers, we paid for what we were.

crane

Why exert myself without a cause?
I'd rather sit and watch the tower crane
outside my city window toward the bridge.
In summer smog that infiltrates the mind,
it's like a ghost, attenuated, gray,
beyond its own particularity.
And later on, at night, it will become
the lonely, red-eyed sentinel I know,
keeping watch above the work it's done,
the work that it will undertake again
when daytime gets to drinking over Queens.
But that is not the point. The tower crane
holds itself apart and does not need
to speak about the nature of its trust.
It makes a pick and puts a load in place
and stands, locked-in, without a narrative.
You too, my crane, will not exert yourself
without a cause, but when you work you move
with ministerial integrity
across the range of your appointed tasks,
a small portfolio of sky events
that you alone are fit to orchestrate.
Imprisoned in triangularities,
you demonstrate a way to rise above
the laws of gravity you work against,
all clearance and capacity and height.
You oversee a tower here, and there,
not asking what is guaranteed to last.
I'm given, now, to you. I only hope

that my line, too, pays cleanly off the sheave
without a hitch, at singular altitude,
the crane block running incorruptibly,
the reeving tight, the lifting taut and true.

blizzard

The blowing snow gives body
to psychotic shapes the wind assumes,
going sixteen ways at once
in a night that's hard to get across.
A New York City bus is stuck,
a snowplow too. The subway's down.
Most everyone is still in bed,
but I put on an overcoat
and go outside to get to work.
On Broadway I'm alone and walk
eleven blocks in the middle lane
at 4:00 a.m., the only place
that's clear enough. The snow is piled
some four feet high and drifting still
in a wind that's only getting worse.
I carry a blackjack going out,
so if there's trouble I at least
won't go to the hospital alone,
but in a blizzard before dawn
no criminals are on the street,
just me and a Nigerian,
Babafemi from Ibadan,
who drives a cab and stops for me
and maybe has a gun somewhere.
We both have promises to keep.

route 17

The ancient evening is distempered
by a brutal wash of luminescence
that is Route 17 during Christmas
—a highway and a holiday well-matched,
a place and time profitably bound
up in a storm of white light and commerce:
Tool Town, Bennigan's, Filene's
Basement. December's overhead
split by Boeing 747s
headed for Newark, I could hardly hear
the frantic conversation in my ear
as we sat in traffic under ten
Santas on top of a Plymouth dealer's
roof, their big hands turned up to heaven.

cross and sphere

Of course they'll never meet, but there they are,
Jesus on the East Side, crucified,
and Atlas on the West Side, leaning in,
each one reconciled by now, we hope,
not only to his awful punishment
but to facing off across Fifth Avenue
halfway down the block from 51st.
Both have graduated from the school
of universal treachery and pain
and find themselves in mid-Manhattan now.
Deep inside St. Patrick's, like a jewel,
Jesus hangs professionally on the cross,
and when the giant front doors open up,
you can see the Son of Man above the throng
of Japanese and widowers from the Bronx
and matrons in a flush of godliness.
Right across the street in a perfect line
is mighty Atlas, lost in his own world
and looking like Mussolini just a tad
but shouldering the heavens like a man
with a second mortgage and child support to pay.
He cannot fail. He's almost falling off
his pedestal, or is he climbing up?
His eyes are hard and empty, like a bird's,
bereft of individuality,
so what he thinks of Christ across the way
is anybody's guess. A reprobate?
Another bleeder in the pantheon?
And what goes through the mind of Jesus Christ
sorrowing down that long cathedral aisle?
He's dwarfed a bit by all the opulence.

Each of them is far too occupied
with his own travails to care too much about
the one who suffers in proximity.
The least that we can do now is to pause
(we played them false a long time ago)
and think about their brands, the cross and sphere.
We cannot really say that they compete,
though Christ the Carpenter upon his wood
has surely taken market share away
from Atlas of the Titanomachy.
Laboring over there on the West Side,
holding up the sky—for what, the birds?
—Atlas cannot ever be redeemed,
and if he prays at all, he prays to be
beyond instead of under everything.

bile

i

My thing is kind of like, you know, the lie,
the lure of personal productivity,
with many of my friends exhausted now.
It's sort of bad. It's really sort of bad.
My sense of self, at best, is notional.
The gurus and consultants charge a fee
and talk about the management of time,
while back at home their kids are smoking weed,
their wives involved in multiple affairs,
upended by the darker urgencies.
I've been to all their seminars, but still
I think a lot about futility
and what to do when everything goes wrong.
I walk my dog and like a glass of wine.

ii

I have no action plan if things go wrong,
and neither do my friends, exhausted now,
upended by the darker urgencies.
The gurus and consultants charge their fees.
Their wives, embroiled in multiple affairs,
have figured out the management of time.
It's sort of bad. It's really sort of bad.
There is no future in futility.
My thing is kind of like, you know, the lie.
I walk my dog and like a glass of wine.
The path of personal productivity
is long. I go to seminars, but still
my sense of self, at best, is notional,
and back at home the kids are smoking weed.

iii

Some wives, I'm told, have multiple affairs
and do not go to seminars, but still
they speak of personal productivity
and methods for the management of time.
What do we do when everything goes wrong?
It's sort of bad. It's really sort of bad.
Perhaps your sense of self is notional?
For me, I walk my dog and drink some wine.
The gurus and consultants charge their fees
to friends of mine, who are exhausted now
and think too much about futility,
while back at home the kids are smoking weed.
My thing is kind of like, you know, the lie.
I can't forget the darker urgencies.

iv

I'm rather given to futility
when so much in my life is notional.
My thing is kind of like, you know, the lie.
I think about the managers of time
upended by the darker urgencies
along their paths of personal productivity.
I walk my dog and like a glass of wine.
My many friends, they are exhausted now,
and some are having multiple affairs,
while back at home the kids are smoking weed.
It's sort of bad. It's really sort of bad
when everything imaginable goes wrong.
The gurus and consultants charge their fees.
I've been to twenty seminars, but still . . .

v

The cost of personal productivity
is sort of bad. It's really sort of bad.
Consultants from Connecticut raise the fee
while back at home their kids are smoking weed,
upended by the darker urgencies.
I cogitate upon futility
and walk my dog and drink a glass of wine.
It's what I do when everything goes wrong.
I've been to all the seminars, and still
the wives are having multiple affairs.
They've learned from gurus how to manage time.
My sense of self, at best, is notional,
and friends of mine, they are exhausted now.
My thing is kind of like, you know, the lie.

cost

I have an asset on my books that I
must carry and maintain despite the cost:
this body that I live in like a house,
a standalone for which I hold the deed.
Despite the cash invested, I have seen
nothing but diminishing returns.
The value goes in one direction, down,
and divest I cannot do. I'd like to find
a venture capitalist who'd look at me
with a klieg light of profit in his eyes,
or her eyes, but everyone's aware
that monies put here aren't recoverable.
My marketing budget swells with every year,
as what I have to advertise becomes
harder to find a market for. Demand
is correlated perfectly with time,
inversely so, as you might have guessed,
and the graph of the relationship is clear
in its predictability. At least
predictability is good, as those
whose job it is to manage risk will say.
They also advise we take into account
a worst-case scenario. Well, fine.
That's the only one I've got, as far
as I can see, so planning for it won't
be complicated, options will be few,
and returns on the investment I have made
won't keep my beneficiaries up
at night fighting over who gets what.
The thing I have will just depreciate,
the net effect of which will likely be

not foreclosure or eviction but
a rendering of my house unlivable,
an act of God that leaves me in the cold
zeroing out my balance in the books.

i entertained a thought

I entertained a thought the other night
that I would say goodbye, at last, to poetry
and start again. How easy life would be
without the self-abusive need to write.
No more the hollowed eyes, no more the fight
to justify what still is left of me.
I'd undertake some work the world could see,
and I would be remunerated right.
But then I took a sip of rye and thought
of all my demons nightly coming round
to sit with me because I'm here, alive,
with so much unresolved. It's what I've bought
and sold they ask of me. It is the sound
they make that I must render to survive.

Notes

Alan Kurdi (page 5)

Alan Kurdi was a three-year-old Syrian boy of Kurdish descent who drowned in the Mediterranean with other members of his family. They were refugees fleeing hardship in their country. His small corpse washed up on a beach in Turkey. The image of his body was memorialized in a photograph by Turkish journalist Nilüfer Demir.

Making War, Into the Mountains, Under Fire, Cordite, Clip, and Concussion Grenades (pages 9-15)

These poems were written by a civilian who has never experienced combat. My father, an Englishman, served in World War II. He was injured by shrapnel in a Stuka attack and subsequently captured by the Germans in Belgium. He spent most of the war in a German POW camp at the Bleicherode salt mine, in the state of Thuringia. My uncle, an American, fought in the Korean War. I have also spoken at some length with veterans who endured combat in Iraq. Based on what I learned from them (my father, my uncle, recent veterans) and through extensive readings on military history and contemporary warfare, I have tried to project myself, through informed imagination, into the minds of those who fought. My aim was to do this with sympathy and respect. Some details in these poems are taken from a book issued by the US military called *Soldier's Manual of Common Tasks, Warrior Skills*, published by the US Army in 2006. I am grateful to all who serve.

One Hundred Pounds of Myrrh (page 21)

This poem is based on Mary's encounter with Jesus after the resurrection, when she mistakes him at night for the gardener (The Gospel According to Saint John, 20:14-16). It was commissioned by Joyce Polistena.

The Stinker (page 32)

This poem refers to Rodin's sculpture *The Thinker*.

The Partridge Family (page 35)

The quoted line in this poem was taken directly from a 1991 AP news wire report entitled "Former Child Star Arrested for Allegedly Beating Transvestite Prostitute."

It's Not OK (page 40)

This is based on an anagram of the phrase "I get it, but it's not OK."

Going Mad (page 41)

I have never gone mad. The poem is pure speculation. I point this out because some have expressed concern.

The Museum of Sex, section x (page 56)

The line "After such knowledge, what forgiveness?" was borrowed from "Gerontion" by T.S. Eliot.

The Bank (page 65)

This is an acrostic. The letters running down the left side of the poem spell out Bear Stearns JPM. Bear Stearns collapsed and was subsumed by JPM (JP Morgan) during the financial crisis in 2008.

Cross and Sphere (page 70)

On Fifth Avenue in New York City, when the front doors of St. Patrick's Cathedral are open, it becomes evident that the image of Jesus on the cross, rising behind the altar, lines up perfectly with the sculpture across Fifth Avenue of Atlas holding up the world in front of Rockefeller Center. It is as though they are looking at each other.

Bile (pages 72-76)

The genesis of this poem was an article I read online about a so-called time-management guru who achieved great success conducting seminars around the country while his family back home was falling apart.

Acknowledgments

I would like to thank the editors of the following publications and websites, where these poems first appeared, sometimes in slightly different versions:

Alabama Literary Review: "Alan Kurdi," "Contemplative," "Funeral," "Going Mad," "Gollum," "Out of Body," "Report Card," "The Stinker," and "Wheelbarrow"

Angle: "Cross and Sphere"

Cimarron Review: "Under Fire," "Clip," "Concussion Grenades," and "Cordite" (from the sequence "The Book of Common Tasks")

The Dark Horse: "The Veery" and "Unlocking the Incredible Power of Small Stones"

Ducts: "It Is What It Is" and *"The Partridge Family"*

The Hopkins Review: "The Museum of Sex"

KIN: "Blizzard"

Literary Matters: "Bile," "Boxer Shorts," "Coyotes," "One Hundred Pounds of Myrrh," "The Bank," and "The Payment Plan"

The New Criterion: "Cost," "Long Live Rock," and "Route 17"

Parnassus: Poetry in Review: "Cup"

The Raintown Review: "Headless Barbie Commission" and "Night Riff"

"The Television Set" was included in *Rabbit Ears: TV Poems* (NYQ Books), edited by Joel Allegretti.

"Headless Barbie Commission" was reprinted in *The Best of The Raintown Review*.

I am indebted to J. Allyn Rosser, who chose my manuscript for the 2020 Donald Justice Poetry Prize, and to Christine Stroud, Mike Good, Shelby Newsom, and Chiquita Babb at Autumn House Press, who brought this book into being. I'm grateful to the Spencer family, who sponsor the Iris N. Spencer Poetry Awards of the West Chester University Poetry Center, including the Donald Justice Poetry Prize. I would also like to thank these friends, who have helped me with my work over the years, either directly or indirectly: Joel Allegretti, Peter Balakian, Ned Balbo, Patricia Behrens, Meredith Bergmann, Shaune Bornholdt, Kim Bridgford,

Stephen Brockwell, Dan Brown, Michael Brown, Gerry Cambridge, Chris Childers, Terese Coe, Henri Cole, Alfred Corn, Eleanor Cory, Paula Deitz, Ben Downing, Caitlin Doyle, Ann Drysdale, Rhina P. Espaillat, Anna M. Evans, George Green, Sam Gwynn, Rachel Hadas, Ernest Hilbert, Stephen Kampa, Julie Kane, David M. Katz, Adam Kirsch, Quincy R. Lehr, Herb Leibowitz, Amy Lemmon, David Mason, William Matthews, Josh Mehigan, Alfred Nicol, Eric Norris, Ken Norris, Uche Ogbuji, Eric Ormsby, Dan Pope, Philip Quinlan, Wendy Sloan, Willard Spiegelman, Timothy Steele, Linda Stern, Luke Stromberg, Bill Thompson, Peter Van Toorn, Ryan Wilson, Anton Yakovlev, and David Yezzi. Finally and forever, I thank Majô, who knows where these poems came from and without whom I would probably not be here.

About the Author

JOHN FOY's third book of poems, *No One Leaves the World Unhurt*, won the 2020 Donald Justice Poetry Prize. His second book, *Night Vision*, won the New Criterion Poetry Prize and was published by St. Augustine's Press in 2016. It was also a finalist for the 2018 Poets' Prize. His first book is *Techne's Clearinghouse*. His work has been included in the *Swallow Anthology of New American Poets*, *The Best of The Raintown Review*, and *Rabbit Ears: TV Poems*. He has published widely in journals, including *The New Yorker*, *Poetry*, *The Hudson Review*, *The New Criterion*, *The Village Voice*, *Parnassus*, *American Arts Quarterly*, *Alabama Literary Review*, *The Dark Horse*, *The Yale Review*, *Barrow Street*, and *The Hopkins Review*. His poems have appeared online in *Literary Matters*, *Poetry Daily*, *Ducts*, *KIN*, *The Nervous Breakdown*, *Big City Lit*, and *Angle*. His essays and reviews have run in *Parnassus*, *The New Criterion*, *Contemporary Poetry Review*, *The Dark Horse*, and other publications, and he has been a guest blogger for *Best American Poetry*. He lives and works in New York.

New and Forthcoming Releases

No One Leaves the World Unhurt by John Foy ◆ Winner of the 2020 Donald Justice Poetry Prize, selected by J. Allyn Rosser

Lucky Wreck: Anniversary Edition by Ada Limón

In the Antarctic Circle by Dennis James Sweeney ◆ Winner of the 2020 Autumn House Rising Writer Prize, selected by Yona Harvey

Creep Love by Michael Walsh

The Dream Women Called by Lori Wilson

"American" Home by Sean Cho A. ◆ Winner of the 2020 Autumn House Chapbook Prize, selected by Danusha Laméris

Under the Broom Tree by Natalie Homer

Molly by Kevin Honold ◆ Winner of the 2020 Autumn House Fiction Prize, selected by Dan Chaon

The Animal Indoors by Carly Inghram ◆ Winner of the 2020 CAAPP Book Prize, selected by Terrance Hayes

speculation, n. by Shayla Lawz ◆ Winner of the 2020 Autumn House Poetry Prize, selected by Ilya Kaminsky

All Who Belong May Enter by Nicholas Ward ◆ Winner of the 2020 Autumn House Nonfiction Prize, selected by Jaquira Díaz

For our full catalog please visit: http://www.autumnhouse.org